A Florence Diary

A Florence Diary

DIANA ATHILL

GRANTA

Granta Publications, 12 Addison Avenue, London W11 4QR

First published in Great Britain by Granta Books 2016

Copyright © Diana Athill 2016

Image on p.20 © SSPL/Getty Images. 2 October 1948. British Railways West Country
Class 4-6-2 steam locomotive No 34039 'Boscastle' at Dover with the Golden
Arrow cross-Channel boat train service, by Reverend Arthur Cawston. Image on
p.29 © Alinari Archives/Villani Archive, Florence, Italy/Bridgeman Images. Ponte
Vecchio, Florence, c.1955, Villani, Achille (1870–1945). Image on p.33 © akg-images/
Mondadori Portfolio. Piazza della Signoria and Palazzo Vecchio, Florence, 1950s.
Image on p.37 © akg-images/Mondadori Portfolio. Man pushing cart between Borgo
San Jacopo and via dello Sprone. Behind him, a greengrocery and the Fountain
of Sprone by Bernardo Buontalenti. Florence, 1950s. Image on p.43 © akg-images
/ Mondadori Portfolio. Women crossing via dei Bardi in front of a café. Florence,
1950s. Image on p.46 © Vincenzo Balocchi/Alinari Archives, Florence/Alinari
via Getty Images. Pigeons on the edge of a fountain. Italy c.1950. Image on p.51 ©
Herbert List/Magnum Photos. Italy, Lemonade Seller, Naples, 1949. Image on p.55 ©
Fratelli Alinari Museum Collections/Balocchi Archive, Florence/Bridgeman Images.
An avenue in the Giardino di Boboli, Palazzo Pitti, Florence, c.1960, Balocchi,
Vincenzo (1892–1975). Image on p.58 © Werner Bischof/Magnum Photos. Cagliari
market, Sardinia, 1950. Image on p.65 © Nigel Goodman/Getty Images. Basilica of
Saint Mary of the Flower, Florence (Basilica di Santa Maria dei Fiori).

A CIP catalogue record for this book
is available from the British Library.

3 5 7 9 10 8 6 4 2

ISBN 978 1 78378 316 8
eISBN 978 1 78378 317 5

Typeset in Minion by M Rules
Printed and bound by CPI Group (UK) Ltd, Croydon, CR0 4YY

MIX
Paper from
responsible sources
FSC
www.fsc.org   FSC® C020471

In loving memory
of my mother
and of dear Pen

INTRODUCTION

❧

Holidays

'Keep a diary for me,' said my mother. So I did, the only one I ever wrote, and she preserved it. Here it is, rescued from the tattered little copybook in which I wrote it, and the sometimes near illegibility of my scrawl. My mother didn't just read it, but even edited it a little: tiny corrections in her handwriting occur here and there. My first excursion abroad to Florence, a gift to me and my cousin Pen from my mother's elder sister, Joyce, to celebrate the end of World War II, was an Event for her as well as for me. I, of course, was thrilled by this wonderful gift, but I'm not sure I fully recognised its significance. I only gradually came to understand how impossible it is to exaggerate the importance of holidays, those two or three weeks every year when I escaped into what felt like real life.

That is not to say that the fifty-odd years I spent as a publisher living in London meant nothing: they were my *raison d'être* as well as the source of my bread and butter, but they didn't answer my dreams. Holidays were seen by some of my friends as romantic chapters in love affairs, but not by me. My holidays left a love affair behind. For most of the time I was living with a moneyless man who drew the line at holidaying at my expense (and anyway claimed to see no point in visiting new places). What I was after was not a shared experience, but the excitement of discovery. I was hungry for the thrill of being elsewhere.

It was this that took me abroad. Only recently did I see how much of my own country I failed to discover because to me a holiday meant foreign travel. France, Italy, Greece, Yugoslavia (as it was then), the Caribbean, the USA – I fell madly in love with places in all these. I remember tears in my eyes when I realised, on leaving Trinidad, that I would probably never again hear the voice of the kiskadee – the bird whose call sounds so exactly like someone asking plaintively, '*Qu'est-ce qu'il dit? Qu'est-ce qu'il dit?*' In Port of Spain it called all day long, until night fell and the barking of dogs took over. And outside the city, frogs. Don't expect much silence in the tropics.

'Abroad' was more enticing than the UK because it was more of an escape after the cruel bottling up of six years of war. Nowhere here could you wake up on a train that had stopped in the middle of the night, push a blind aside, and see a lantern carried along an unknown platform by a man talking to another in an unknown language – those voices, the tiny glimpse of foreign ordinariness giving you such a tingle of excitement. And next morning, if you were Italy-bound – *mountains* sailing by, and look! A white streak – a *waterfall*! Train journeys were more exciting than flights were going to be, and more comfortable if you could afford a bunk (only rarely did I rise to the luxury of a proper sleeper; more often I was sitting up as we did on that first journey). Just once did I experience the perfect way of travelling; driving your car onto first boat, then train, where (you were in France by now) you ate an amazingly good dinner in the station buffet before strolling to find your sleeper. Next morning, way down south, you were served breakfast on the train, then watched your car being run off its carrier, and tootled off at your leisure. You could do this going to Scotland, too – but not for long: too expensive, I suppose.

Arrivals included the identifying of smells. All countries have their smells (France's used to be Gauloises tobacco, drains and coffee), enjoyable simply for being theirs. (To be honest, Scotland has the best smell, and you must arrive by air to get it – but I didn't know that at the time of my early holidays.)

I learned to like travelling alone because you connect with strangers much better that way, but to begin with I usually went with a cousin. Cousins are the best for intimacy. Brothers and sisters are too close and friends ... we had a good many friends, but none – and I wonder whether this is a very English thing? – none with whom we could talk about things that *really mattered*. Whereas with my beloved cousins – no problem! Pen, the cousin with whom I went to Florence in this diary, was the nearest to me in age. We could hardly have been more different from one another but we travelled together as comfortably as a pair of old bedroom slippers.

She was armed with a touching naivety which made her bolder than I was in many ways. I shall never forget the amazement on the faces of a room full of Italian businessmen when, having walked the length of a street asking everyone, '*Dov'è il Signor Amico?*' (I trailing her but busily pretending not to know her) she finally hit on his office and demanded that he give her better terms than a bank would have done for her pounds sterling. He paid up. (I can't remember who had told Pen about him.) She also got herself shown round

4

Bernard Berenson's marvellous house, Villa I Tatti, which I hadn't the nerve even to think of attempting. (Some years later Pen underwent an intense spiritual experience at Assisi, and became a Catholic – finally a very happy nun.)

It was to another cousin that I owe my other lovely Italian holidays: my cousin Toby, who bought a house near Lucca in which I stayed for six consecutive summer holidays. It was a large but simple farmhouse converted by a citizen of Lucca sometime in the eighteen-hundreds into his country villa. With his own hand he had painted the walls of his *salone* with scenes from the novels of Walter Scott, adding a frieze of carefully imagined 'family portraits' into the bargain. It was the oddest mixture of attempted grandeur and naughtiness. Toby bought the house from two old ladies who became so flustered when asked to remove its contents that they ended by begging him to keep the lot, so when I opened a drawer in my favourite bedroom out fell a bundle of Latin exercises written by a little boy in 1883, and a very long ode to the opening of the first tramway in Lucca. The bathroom attached to that bedroom took a bit of getting used to, because on its window was painted an appalling but convincing red-whiskered footman, leering at whoever was in the bath.

An astonishing thing about that house was that whenever something was needed, it turned up. Having dug out a swimming pool at the bottom of its large and beautiful garden, Toby saw that ideally there should be a stone mask out of which the water could gush into the pool. Three days later just such a mask turned up in the potting shed, and he hardly felt surprised, so often did such things happen. It was a house in which happy years were spent, and I was lucky to see so much of it.

Naturally the charm of a place often depends on its inhabitants as well as on its beauty and intrinsic interest. Dominica, in the Eastern Caribbean, for example, an exceptionally lovely island where rainforested mountains plunge so abruptly into the sea that no road can be built to encircle it, is coloured by being Jean Rhys's island even long after her death. She was 'my' author for the last fifteen years of her life – very much so, because if ever a writer needed nannying because of practical ineptitude, Jean was that writer, and like it or not you became firmly linked to her. You liked it, in fact, because however maddening Jean sometimes was, she had the charm (as well, of course, as the genius) to counteract it. So getting to know the island that had meant so much to her, meant a great deal to me, the more so because her reputation

in Dominica is in the hands of Lennox Honychurch, probably the most interesting and likeable man in the whole
Caribbean, who, with his mother Patricia, became the most
generous of friends. Patricia had built a little house in her
garden – her handsome botanical garden designed by her
daughter – which she sometimes let to tourists and in which
she firmly established me as a guest. It took me less than a
day to feel at home.

Indeed, I felt more than at home. I remember leaning on
the counter of the local police station, waiting for my driving licence to be made valid on the island, listening to the
creaking of the ceiling fan and watching the lazy circling of
the flies, and being suddenly seized by the most powerful
sensation of *belonging*: surely I had known this place all my
life. And I allowed myself to imagine that a deeply buried
Caribbean gene had been activated. Because Athills had,
in fact, moved from Norfolk to the West Indies, probably
when the once very profitable wool trade went off the boil
so that young men had to seek their livings further afield.
They had settled in Antigua as sugar planters, and done
embarrassingly well (embarrassing not to them, but to
descendants uncomfortably aware of how many slaves they
must have employed). One of them, (I can't remember how

many 'greats' there are in our relationship) became one of the island's leading citizens and was so pompously proud of his family that he kept a detailed record of it, which eventually came into my brother's hands.

My brother was interested enough to study it, and noticed something odd. The man who, it seemed, must have been our direct ancestor, disappeared. If he had died it would have been recorded: he was just *gone*. Had he, perhaps, blotted his copybook in some way? My sister-in-law, who enjoys family histories and has a streak of the bloodhound in her, wrote to Antigua's chief librarian and asked if anyone existed who knew a lot about Antigua's social history. She was sent an address and followed it up. And lo! Our man had indeed blotted his copybook. He had married his mistress, and his mistress was – shock! horror! – one-sixteenth black. You need to know a great deal about West Indian attitudes to race in the past to understand the significance of that (one would think) wholly trivial fact. Every conceivable degree of blackness, down to the invisible, carried a derogatory label (I forget the label for one-sixteenth, but it existed), and every degree was abominated and despised. So my ancestor was Unforgiveable – and was also, hurrah hurrah, the only sensible and honourable Athill in

Antigua! I only wish that my teeny-weeny shadow of a black gene really was making itself felt, but fear that it is most unlikely. The feeling of 'home' was probably Dominica's seductiveness at work. I've never met any visitor to it who has not succumbed.

Such a feeling is not essential to the enjoyment of a place: Florence didn't feel like home. Its great charm lay in its unlikeness to home – in its being so enchantingly 'elsewhere'. And I am forever grateful that it was my very first 'elsewhere'. None could be lovelier. I visited it only once more before its popularity began to make it so exhausting that other cities became preferable. I don't know how it is that Venice, just as swamped by tourists as poor Florence, manages to shrug them off so much more successfully.*

On my second visit I was a guest, which was interesting but deprived me of the element of freedom. I was staying with Eduardo, a cousin's cousin who had a job with NATO, which

---

* In fact I do know. To Venice they are fed in by busloads and each load has to stick together behind its shepherd who keeps it strictly to the main piazza and streets. They are scared to lose touch with their bus – what if they were abandoned? Go five yards down a side street, and you are free of them. In Florence they wander free and uncontrolled – or more nearly so. It makes all the difference. And of course, in Florence, there's the parking problem, which Venice spares you.

seemed to be teaching Americans not to be uncouth when compared to Italians. He didn't appear to be making much headway against the tide of alcohol on which the Americans were floating.

Eduardo had rented an elegant flat from a woman to whom he was related, and was in a condition of dismay because some weeks earlier she had asked him if she might return to her flat for a few days, and *she was still there*, accompanied by a pregnant cocker spaniel which had been established in the dining room. The poor dog was never taken for walks and had to use the balcony as its lavatory. Even worse, the housekeeper had now reverted to answering the telephone with 'Signora X's residence', not Eduardo's name. Eduardo was much too polite to say anything about all this, except in a hushed wail to me, and I was not able to offer much encouragement. My money would have been on that woman any day.

Eduardo was particularly anxious because he had planned, very kindly, a dinner party in my honour, and I need hardly say that the puppies began to be born in the dining room that very day – and not only did the birth begin, but it proved to be a difficult one, which meant that I was called into play because being British, surely I must know all about dogs. I managed eventually to shift the task onto the shoulders of the vet, and joined Eduardo in furiously scrubbing the floor of the balcony, where dinner would have to be served. We were able to find a vase big enough to cover the drain-hole and contain the smells.

I was called to the dining room only twice during dinner and all the six puppies survived, but I don't think Eduardo's nerves ever quite recovered. The woman and her dog were still there when I left, and the last I heard of their reluctant host was that he had moved to Sicily.

That was the only one of my many holidays which prevents me from saying they were *all* perfect. Apart from that one, what a record of escape, discovery, renewal and refreshing plunges into what I most wanted to experience. I marvel at my luck.

It would be difficult – probably impossible – to convey by words on paper the reality of the places and incidents that I enjoyed so much. I can only make a few token attempts. A terrace high up in a Corfiot olive orchard, the trees huge and distorted because it was not the local habit to discipline them, a donkey braying a long way off, its voice might have been the sound of baking sunlight, and down below a sea through which that sunlight seemed to fall in a network of gold where a little old boat lay on its emerald shadow. I lay on that terrace all afternoon without wanting to move, just looking, looking . . .

An evening, late in a Dubrovnik bar, gipsies playing. 'The gipsies know me well' – 'I hate their music' – 'So do I, but they trust me.' And later he said, 'My father died – a natural death,' and I looked round that room – so many gaunt faces – those over there despise us – and understood that very recently a 'natural death' had indeed been worthy of remark. It was so strange – the intensity still steaming off the violent past, the colour it was giving to an amusing flirtation in a very lovely place. 'Look at me, dancing with an *English general's daughter*!' a Russian friend of his had crowed earlier in the evening (he was dancing with my cousin), and we had all laughed and laughed.

The sound – the distant sound of a steel band coming nearer and nearer through the darkness: *J'ouvert*, first day of Trinidad's Carnival, sleepiness so early in the morning as the bands gathered, and then the almost incredible blaze of colour and invention going on all day, sleepiness surely forgotten for ever until at midnight the music stopped and everyone fell down. Crash bang, down they went, no longer held up by the music. And all those magical costumes littering the gutters (though some were rescued). What a day, what a day!

In Dominica there was a place where earth bubbled. Oh yes, they said, it will blow sooner or later, look at the Boiling Lake. To do that you had to take a three-hour mountain walk, and it was a scary sight, that huge crater full of boiling whatever-it-is that was contained so precariously under our feet. A whiff of its steaming might kill you – had killed people. It did blow, long ago, changing the island's whole shape, and the tremors people are now used to give a frightening edge of danger to its rich rainforest beauty. I bought a bag of mud at the bubbly place (for the complexion, they said, but I never tried it) and I also held a boa constrictor in my arms, and felt it squeeze me, protesting at being held – a steady and impressive sensation. Had I been smaller it would have been alarming. The man who caught the boa had broken the law, and I should have walked off with it into the forest and let it go, but chickened out at the prospect of offending him and the group of villagers surrounding us. It was not a big boa, but handsome. Though less marvellous than the thousands of fireflies filling the forest that night, weaving a silent web of glittering lust. It was the perfect silence of all that feverish activity that was uncanny, leaving us spellbound.

In New Mexico – the champagne freshness of desert air made breathing a new joy even in Santa Fe, though that town, all adobe (or sham adobe) is so unlike other American cities that its not smelling towny is natural. It was full of lilacs in flower, and disconcertingly its streets often became rambling roads, houses standing back behind gardens. And what looked like houses might be shops, or more often galleries. We felt timid at entering them and sometimes more so once inside. The charm of Santa Fe had caused us to expect tourist bait, but here was sometimes the finest of fine art. 'That can't – that surely *can't* be a Rembrandt,' we would think. But it was! Because these galleries, or some of them, catered for Texan millionaires. But what was odd and pleasant was that relaxed surroundings produced relaxed people. Those running the galleries were as welcoming to two obviously unrich tourists as to any rich man. Perhaps if you serve millionaires you don't actually *see* an ordinary person very often, so it is maybe quite enjoyable when one happens to walk in. Certainly we were shown some marvellous things, and had a memorable time. And in the less grand but still fine shops we bought some rings which we still liked when we got them home – something quite unusual with holiday buys.

But the strangest New Mexican experience was driving along a dead-straight flat-as-a-table road stretching, it seemed, for ever, and suddenly seeing two little gate posts. On reaching them – screech of brakes and, indeed, screech of human voice. Before us was a Void. The ground fell away so abruptly and so far that we were looking down on the backs of swallows who were catching insects above the tiny Rio Grande which had carved out this gigantic gorge. Driving across the narrow bridge which began at the gate posts and spanned its terrifying width, I couldn't glance down or vertigo would have won.

Our excursion would take us about fifty miles, and then we would have to cross back to our own side of the gorge, presumably by a similar bridge. But the point reached, there were not even gate posts. There was a gorse bush, and then nothing: the road disappeared over the gorge's rim. And the gorge was just as deep as before.

We got out of the car to peer down in incredulous dismay. Should we turn round and go back to cross by the bridge we'd come over, fifty miles back? But then we heard an approaching vehicle. What eventually appeared below us, clambering beetle-like up the gorge's wall, was a very ancient little truck. When it reached us, and staggered over the rim onto the flat, we saw its driver was an equally ancient man. At that point we had to say: 'If he can do it, we can.'

As a matter of fact, the descent was not difficult. The road was wider than we expected, we could hug the side wall of it, averting our eyes from the drop, and we reached the little bridge across the river (not wide at that point) sooner than we expected. It was the ascent that I remember with horror. It was rockier, the road narrower, very forbidding. The rock was so fiercely black and 'our' side had become the drop side. If we met another car (and we did twice) we either had to cower against the black wall to the approacher's fury, or perch sickeningly on the very edge of the black drop. Fear of such an encounter became as nerve-wracking as the event itself. I have never felt more relieved about anything than reaching the top.

But it was very gratifying to be told that evening that 'not many tourists cross there. Mostly they turn back to the bridge.' Sissies! I wouldn't be remembering the look of that little river (it was *inconceivable* that so small a stream could have carved out that vast gorge, but it had) or those improbable swooping swallows with the clarity I'm now enjoying if we had not pursued that drive to its proper end. Seeing is believing, and we had not just *seen*, but had *driven* the hard-to-believe. And terrifying though it was, it was also huge fun – and not a little smug-making. Because what makes good holidays is not lying on beaches and dipping into delicious seas, or drinking good wine and eating well-cooked meals (though some meals will remain memories to be revered). Such things are the jam spread on bread and butter. It is the quality of the whole thing including the bread and butter which makes the experience important. And that is why I remember Port of Spain's barking dogs, pestilential though they were, almost as fondly as its kiskadees.

I could go on for pages and pages more, but I won't. Holidays are great and holidays end. So now, back to that first experience of magical 'elsewhere' in Florence. Did I ever thank my darling Ma for asking me to record it? I don't think I did, but I am truly grateful to her: I never would have forgotten it, but I couldn't have remembered it so well without the diary. May you all have lots of holidays as good as that one.

Bon voyage!

Diana Athill
April 2016

A Florence Diary

Sunday, 24 August 1947

The Golden Arrow left Victoria at eight in the morning, so I had to have all my packing absolutely finished the night before, and order the car to the station, as the chance of a taxi at that hour in the morning on a Sunday was very slim. Pen stayed the night at the station hotel. I arrived early and registered my suitcase through, so that I didn't have to bother with it at all. I took with me only a hatbox with odds and ends, and a shopping bag with masses of food for the journey. We had seats reserved, second-class, but no sleepers. Pen didn't register any luggage, and although her stuff was small it was very numerous, and largely tied together with insecure pieces of string. It included a smart white straw hat with blue veil, a collection of canvases, and a vicious easel which poked people in the eye at every move and kept on losing legs.

Victoria to Folkestone was dull, but Folkestone to Boulogne was glorious. The Channel was truly blue for once, and glittering, and there was enough wind to keep us cool but not enough to make us sick. We stayed up in front of the boat, watching for France. It was incredible that anyone should have been seasick, but we know for a fact that at least one person was, because when we reclaimed our luggage we found that they had done it over Pen's case.

The train to Paris was luxurious – like English first class. There was a funny couple with us, who had a noisy but nice baby of about two. She was Birmingham and he was Bordeaux, and she talked English all the time and he talked French all the time and they understood each other perfectly although neither of them could utter a word of the other's language. The baby, not unnaturally, was turning out a late speaker.

We crossed from the Gare du Nord to the Gare de Lyons, with great aplomb, by bus. (Pen's inspiration – I'm better at travelling than she is when it comes to luggage, but she has the greater resourcefulness.) We had four hours in Paris. We ambled about, and dined very pleasantly somewhere near the Jardin des Plantes. We each had about two pounds worth of francs, but after dinner and porters and left luggage and the bus, it was nearly all gone. France is definitely not a place for a holiday now.

The Simplon-Orient-Express left at nine something. It was less luxurious, and full. Some amiable people suddenly took Pen under their wing and decided that by moving a reservation card, they could get her a corner seat in the next carriage, so she went off. I was left with an Italian girl who was busily suckling her three-month-old baby (she was called Mrs Bisset and had been living in Liverpool, but she couldn't talk any English either), an Italian jeweller with a very peevish sixteen-year-old son, who never spoke or ate for all the journey, a very old and peasanty Italian woman with a sweet and surprisingly well-off daughter, and my Roman prince. I didn't know he was a prince at that stage. The girl with the baby smelt of sweat and the jeweller smelt of garlic, and I felt that the night would be rather dreadful. It was, as long as one tried to sleep, because sleeping sitting up is such hell, but actually we didn't try to sleep much. Alfonso (the prince) spoke good English and had just been over in London and Cambridge on a student's tour. He was extraordinarily nice – corduroy trousers and knapsack – and of an extremely sociable disposition, and had a passion for exercising his English. About twenty-five, I should say, and nice looking in a not particularly Italian way. We reached the frontier by about six, and after all the fuss with the *douane* (during which a rather odd lady in Pen's carriage was searched all over and I almost had to pay for my cigarettes only Alfonso quickly explained that I was with him and half of them were his) it was impossible to try to doze any more. So I went and had breakfast with and paid for by Alfonso, and Pen felt rather sad for a short time. Then we had a lovely time watching Switzerland. It was a little misty and not too hot, thank God. When we arrived at Domodossola Pen and I and Alfonso went and had coffee and sponge fingers, and she relented towards him a little. We were terribly dirty by that time.*

Once in Italy the corridors filled up, because they are so short of rolling stock that they have to use the continental expresses as local trains. We all bobbed up and down exclaiming with patriotic fervour at all the sights, particularly Lake Maggiore, and when we got to the flat part I went and had lunch with (and on) Alfonso.

At Milan we had an hour or two and we had to go to Cooks because, although we had through tickets, we had not got through reservations. Alfonso took us there. Then we went to have baths in a hotel (Pen's inspiration), and surprisingly

---

* In steam trains smuts blew in through the windows.

enough, Alfonso didn't actually bath us. Pen panicked because she thought the train left at five, and got cross with Alfonso again, because he kept on saying, 'Don't fuss, it's five thirty' (which, of course, it was). I got on to a tram to go back to the station, and the doors shut before they could follow me, and I was swept off and suddenly realised that, not having yet changed a traveller's cheque, I had not one single lira on me. A kind lady paid my fare amid much laughter. We all joined up safely on the train, and found it *packed,* but the jeweller had fought tooth and nail and kept our seats free. The old lady and her daughter had been replaced by a fine figure of an elderly man and a little boy who slept so soundly that even when I spilt a bottle of Evian over him he never stirred. The Italian girl's baby was by this time almost in a stupor, because whenever it *stirred* she thrust her nipple into its mouth, and in between times she danced it up and down like a mad thing, and everyone poked it all the time. Its dirty nappies were hung on the rack to dry and then used again. The poor girl had brought no food, but everyone did pretty well by her.

Shortly after Milan I had dinner with (and on) Alfonso. Pen came along and joined us after a while, because a certain amount of vino was circulating in her carriage by that time, and the stout gentleman kept inviting her to sit on his knee.

When we all went back, he sang her Piedmontese love songs, clasping her hands in both his, and Alfonso discreetly said that he couldn't translate Piedmontese. Alfonso couldn't sing, but painstakingly translated to me all the words of all the songs he could remember, and large bits of Dante, too. We were all pretty tired by then, but nothing was going to stop him exercising his English. (We'd discovered his princely extraction at Milan, which was where we first exchanged names. His card was magnificently embossed with crowns, which he quickly scribbled out, blushing. He was called Caracciolo di Forino).

We reached Florence at midnight (*forty* hours), and dear Alfonso found us a porter and quelled the easel, and told us the black market exchange rate for the last time, and said we must, *must* come to Rome, and then we parted. The hotel was very near the station, and we *flopped* into bed. My waste-paper basket overflowed with all the food that had gone bad on the journey, in spite of giving it to people.

TUESDAY, 26 AUGUST 1947

At nine thirty there was a knock on my door, and in came the porter with a monstrous bunch of stephanotis, 'To wish you a happy stay – Alfonso'. Pen had one too. When we'd got over our surprise we remembered that at Milan he had suddenly said, 'Excuse me, wait here for two minutes' and darted down a side street. He must have ordered them from a shop which had a branch in Florence, and made them send off the cards by post at *once*. What an *enchanting* race! We are seriously considering going on to Rome!

I had to collect my registered case at the customs during the morning, which involved walking down all the corridors of a sort of barracks at least five times, and paying innumerable officials small fees in exchange for incomprehensible forms. Before that we had changed cheques. Pen vaguely remembered being told that Signor Amico, of via del Campidoglio, gave a good rate of exchange, but she hadn't got his address. I came over very British and timid suddenly, and said don't be silly, how can we find him. Undeterred she plunged down the street, saying to one and all, 'Signor Amico? Signor Amico?' like the 'Gilbert, Gilbert' woman after the Crusades. And sure enough in a restaurant someone said, 'Ah! Signor *D*'Amico!', and leapt up and led us to his door. Actually he only gave us about 500 lire – roughly five shillings – more to the pound than the banks, as the pound, having boomed, is slumping like mad. Still it was something, and rather a triumph.

Then we had to go to the pensione we are going to after three days in this hotel, and see that all was well there. To our enormous joy we found that it is *on* the Arno, and our rooms look half over the river and half over a lovely bosky garden, and that it is charming in every way. It costs about 12s 6d a day with all meals!

Then we lunched in a smart restaurant for the hell of it, and then we went to the Palazzo Pitti and looked at *the* most glorious collection of pictures imaginable until we were so exhausted that we could do no more (we hadn't quite revived from the journey) and after that we got a *permesso* for the Boboli Gardens and meant to rest in them, only we were continually led on by new and wonderful vistas.

We had dinner outside – a less smart restaurant, but good, and a violinist and guitarist came out and played to us all the time because we tipped them *much* too much. A beggar woman came along who was training her child, of about three. She pushed it up to us, and then the idea was that she said to it, 'Come away. Don't annoy the ladies,' whereupon it had to begin to cry and cling to us, thereby winning our hearts. The poor little thing wasn't very good at it yet. We felt beastly not giving anything, but kept remembering all we'd heard about being firm with Italian beggars. There aren't a

great many now. Food is expensive, though, and I'm afraid there is a big gap between rich and poor – but of course, there always was.

The shops have *heavenly* things in them – fairly cheap compared to England, but not very. The recovery is astonishing. There didn't seem to be a bombed building in Milan upon which they weren't working, and they had got it back much nearer to normal than London. Everyone seems pleased to see English people, and very kind and charming. Even the touts aren't a nuisance. We have discovered the technique. If you are British and haughty they go on at you, but if you smile very courteously and say, '*Grazie, grazie*' they stop at once, all smiles, and let you go on.

We went to bed early.

WEDNESDAY, 27 AUGUST 1947

We were late this morning, owing to Pen washing her hair and us both having baths (cold – they have no coal, and a very hot summer has dried up the water supply for electricity. That is their worst trouble now, I think).

I went to Cooks and learnt the hideous news that one can't reserve seats on the return journey. They say first class is not much more expensive, so if I have enough money left I shall go by it. Pen is staying longer. One pays on the train, first in lire then in Swiss francs, then in French francs. Tedious.

Then we wandered, mostly looking at the Palazzo Vecchio. Everything is so beautiful that even not 'doing' anything special is marvellous. We are now eating at the pensione (we move in tomorrow) and had a good lunch there.

We then went to the Accademia di Belle Arti and saw wonderful Michelangelo sculptures and an astounding collection of primitives and two dream-like Botticellis, and a special exhibition of pictures that were wrecked in the war and which they are restoring, with photos of all the different stages. They are working miracles on them. Things that were blistered fragments are made almost whole again. Such skill and patience is almost unbelievable.

Then a most splendid tea, with ices and sponge fingers and little iced cakes that melted in the mouth – one of the things we do saying, 'Just this *once*'.

After that a church – Santa Maria Novella – which had lovely frescos, but badly lit and so dirty that one cannot see the detail at all. There was a lovely conjuror outside, swallowing a sword and doing a very rude trick with a little funnel.

After dinner at the pensione we sat on its loggia, which

is *high* up, and looked over the Arno by moonlight. *Oh* so lovely.

It is being deliciously cool, so that one is just exactly comfortable in a cotton frock. Everyone says, 'What a shame it can't be more sunny', but it is a good thing really. I bought a sun hat in a market this morning simply because I couldn't resist it, but it isn't necessary at the moment. It is huge and rather floppy and striped round and round, dark red and straw coloured.

This hotel (Bonciani) isn't at all bad – big and rambling – but it's not as lovely as the pensione, and it will be fun to get there. Madame Rigatti, who runs it, is young and very pretty and speaks English, and adores Pen's friend who recommended us. Leaving the hotel will be expensive in tips – there are *so* many different servants. Two different liftmen, both of whom are our special friends, a bath lady, and chambermaid, an old man pushing a mop who fetched the vases for our flowers, a waiter, a boy pushing another mop and a cross porter and a nice night porter. We can only hope that they won't all be there. I bet the cross porter is. He rather despises us because he saw our passports which have written in them how much (or how little) money we have got.

I've lost my precious phrase book, so we aren't much good

at sustained conversations, though I find myself surprisingly quick at understanding what they say to me, if it's simple.

Now, having written this diary so far, I must go to bed. The smell of stephanotis is rather drowsy-making.

THURSDAY, 28 AUGUST 1947

We left the Hotel Bonciani this morning, in a shower of gold. From our enormous popularity at the end, we deduce that we must, as usual, have over-tipped like mad. It *is* so difficult to know where you are with lire, what with half a dozen different rates of exchange, and even the 'official' one being artificial. Also the Italians haven't yet caught up with the depreciation of their money, just as we haven't. Half a crown to us still seems quite big, although the Americans, seeing it from outside, know it's only about sixpence. And in the same way 500 lire seems a lot to the average Italian, though it works out at only about three shillings to us.

We brought our things down to the pensione in one of the more decrepit cabs, with a very sad horse. Most of them are rather good nowadays. Remembering stories of how Italians treat animals, I was spying about for atrocities but most of the cabmen I see are busily engaged in giving their horses drinks out of miniature buckets, or bathing their hooves, or whisking flies off them.

Then the hotel rang up to say we had left some things. As Pen had already dropped everything five times, and had had to bob upstairs twice to collect things she'd forgotten and *then* been chased to the cab by a chambermaid clasping two side combs and all her French money, I said, 'Pen! You can jolly well go back by yourself and fetch them,' and flounced off across the river on my own. So it was rather mortifying to discover at lunchtime that although she had indeed left her canvases, she had been handed by the hall-porter, in addition to them, a very squalid suspender belt and a pair of dirty pants of *mine*.

I walked through the rather slummy part, where workmen sit in the doorways busily carpentering genuine antiques – very well too – to a church called Santa Maria del Carmine, which has a chapel with lovely frescoes by Lippi, Masolino and Masaccio, and stayed there until it was shut up at twelve.

We went again after lunch, so that Pen could see them, but it was still shut, so we walked down to the old wall and sat on the bank watching a very nice ferry which seems to be run for the sole entertainment of the ferryman and half a dozen little boys. They pull it back and forth on a wire, fishing the while with rapt devotion, some of them with Heath Robinson multiple rods, and apparently for the purest love of the sport as there is never any sign of anyone catching anything. There was an old man with a cobalt blue hat with long feathers in it, selling them something out of gourds.

Then we pottered back into civilisation and found a wonderful Ghirlandaio fresco in Santa Trinita, with Florence looking just the same in the background.

After that we succumbed to our British instincts and went and had a cup of tea in the English-American Tea Rooms. Then Pen explored some more, but I came back and washed my hair. We had rashly stuck our heads out of the windows of the French train, and became thoroughly be-sooted. After Paris it was electric, and quite clean. As the water was cold, I'm not really much cleaner now.

We had been told that the food here in the pensione would be solid but not exciting, but we find it very delicious indeed, and most copious, and are stuffing to capacity. The best part of the food, though, is the cakery part. The pastry shops are full of the most miraculous little objects, that are as exotic as sweets and not much bigger, but more varied in taste and texture. I could eat them for ever. We never quite know what we will get, either. For instance, when yesterday we ordered

(or thought we ordered) chocolate to drink, with cream on top, we got instead an immense double ice, chocolate and vanilla, which was scrumptious.

I am writing up in the loggia, which is not a bit like the Spacious Loggia at B.H.* It is this sort of house – rather fortress like, and the bottom two floors mysterious and apparently inaccessible, with barred windows, and the top floors inexplicably well lit with huge windows, although from the outside you wouldn't think it.

Nobody seems to use the loggia much, we can't think why. When I came up this evening after dinner, I almost gasped

---

* Reference to home.

at the beauty of it. There is a moon and the sky is velvet blue, and the lights on the hill opposite are reflected in long wavering streaks in the velvet blue Arno – so lovely.

Now we have been joined by an Italian girl who works in a chemist's shop near here, and wants to exercise her English. She has so little, and our Italian is so much less, that we have ended talking in French, to no one's benefit. She is nice – she loves her Italian things so much, like they all do. She has just said that when she went to the Pitti last Sunday she kept touching the pictures so that she could say, 'Now I have touched something that Raphael himself worked on with his own hands'. I am going to the cinema with her one evening.

Pen and I are sharing a room just for this night, as there was a bit of a muddle (caused by us), but tomorrow we move into our sweet little ones over the walled garden.

Friday, 29 August 1947

I had a lovely morning today. Pen went off to see the things I had seen yesterday and vice versa and when I got to San Lorenzo, which she had said was lovely but hadn't anything special in it, I discovered that she had missed the whole *thing* about it, which is that you go through a little door behind one of the altars, and come suddenly into the Chapel of the Medicis. They started to build it to receive the Holy Sepulchre, which they tried to steal, and when the stealing expedition failed, they finished the chapel just in honour of themselves, for their tombs. It's HUGE, octagonal, and entirely lined with precious inlays. It positively stuns one with its magnificence. It isn't a bit to the Glory of God – purely the Medicis saying, 'Look what our family can do if we want to!'

It is rather sombre and utterly overwhelming. All round it are coats of arms of the tributaries of Florence inlaid in great panels on the lowest part of the wall, man-size, and these you can really see close up. They used mother-of pearl and cornelian and coral and chalcedony and agate and porphyry and Heaven knows what, but each design is so sweeping and simple that the effect isn't in the least fussy. At inter- vals round the walls are set vast sarcophagi of red and grey granite, and on each is the crown of the occupant, lying on a stone cushion set with enormous emeralds and rubies and sapphires. The frescoes and things we have been seeing are more lovely really, because they are true artist's work, but this thing is so much Florence, and so full of the splendour of that incredible family, that I think it really excited me more. And next door to it is the chapel Michelangelo built to Lorenzo and Cosimo, with his magnificent memorials to them, and the loveliest of all his virgins.

After that I only just had time to fly round the Bargello before coming back for lunch, and that again is staggering. It is used as a museum for sculpture, and is full of lovely things, but the building itself is what thrilled me. The courtyard, with a colonnade all round and a gallery on the first floor with great stairs coming down, is the most beautiful thing I have ever seen.

We went to Fiesole after lunch, complete with painting things, on a very full tram. The view was misty today, and so enormous that it daunted even Pen, so that we never got down to trying to draw it. We went instead to the Roman amphitheatre, which looks out away from Florence, and is quiet and smells of thyme, and we lay on the grass and relaxed. It was country and peaceful and lovely, and we are going to spend a whole day there soon. It suddenly rained while we were there. The sun still shone and it became no colder, but great fat silver drops came splashing down.

We've decided to buy a villa up there, with an olive orchard and some vines and a couple of fig trees, and have all our friends to stay.

We are so lucky with the weather. The terrible heat wave they have been having really seems to have stopped, and I suppose *they* think it's quite cool, but to us it couldn't be more perfect. One is exactly at the right temperature all the time, without having to think about it – except walking along the Lungarno, at midday, where there is no shade, and then one does cook a bit. We sleep under nothing but sheets and a cotton bedspread.

A large black hen lives on the roof across the garden from me, and while I was cleaning up for dinner there was a sudden descent of finches on to the trees – hundreds of them. They *may* have been sparrows, but if they were they were talking Italian.

SATURDAY, 30 AUGUST 1947 AND
SUNDAY, 31 AUGUST 1947

I forgot to write this up yesterday – and anyway it must be getting rather boring for anyone else to read now, because it is really all 'And then we went – and then we went', and the beauties of Florence hardly need describing. But all the same I'll carry on. Yesterday morning we saw Santa Croce, which has in it the most perfectly preserved (and restored)

frescoes – *heaps* of them – that we have yet seen, some of them by Giotto. They looked so wonderful because for once they were lit, and we happened on the right time of day when the sun was streaming through the right windows, so that the painted walls glowed like ripe peaches. It must have looked more like it did when it was new and brilliant than any of the other churches we have seen, particularly as whole chapels of frescoes are still complete, not just patches here and there.

The afternoon was rather pottery, taken up by trying to get into the Fra Angelico museum (shut for the *third* time) and looking at Pen's shoes. She has only uncomfortable ones with her, and has seen some lovely sandals in the via Cavour, but as they are expensive, she can't make up her mind to buy them. We look at them about once a day. We also bought some nyum nyums at a pastry shop, and had a drink sitting in the Palazzo Vecchio square. We allow ourselves *either* some nyum nyums *or* some fruit every day, as our only expenses beyond an occasional tram fare or entrance money, and sometimes a drink or something in the middle of the afternoon. In the evening there was a thunderstorm, and we sat snugly in the loggia watching it.

I had a letter from Alfonso, offering hospitality in Rome,

which tempted us very much. His family are in the country, and he says we could stay in their flat (I may add that he has one of his own). We don't think we can go, as although we'd gladly eat any amount of meals off him, and let him show us around, we feel that we can't actually *stay* on him, considering that we *did* only meet him on the train, so that the whole expedition would be beyond our means. I had also a p.c. from a friend of mine saying, 'Come to Venice', but I'm afraid that only applies to me and anyway as he's English he would only have a few lire and his hospitality would be limited!

On Sunday (today) we crossed the river and climbed two or three hundred yards of broad shallow steps, between cypresses to San Miniato. There is a great wide space, with a wall round it, looking over the town, and a monastery and a church that is said to have been founded by the first Christians of Florence, in Nero's reign, and it's all olive-orchardy and delicious. That was a heavenly expedition, rather like the Roman amphitheatre one.

Oh yes, and yesterday we went into a little church with a superb ceiling, to see a Filippino Lippi, and there was a little mass going on which was being taken, apparently, by a ragged little boy – there was a priest there for the important

bits – and which was for women and children. It was very
solemn and charming.

After lunch today we talked to a young Swiss sculptor
who is staying here. Unfortunately he leaves tomorrow. He
was rather delightful, and said that he had actually seen with
his own eyes a fish being caught in the Arno, which made
him breathless with excitement – but alas, it fell off the hook
before it was six inches out of the water.

It became terribly hot in the afternoon and our expedition
to the Boboli Gardens, to find a vista for Pen to paint, ended
in us flopping in the shade in the amphitheatre, which is *too*
lush and Renaissance for words, and watching the people.
We've decided that probably the reason for the Italians not
being a very warlike nation is that they are exhausted in early
youth by continual joggling about, and being made to walk
at too early an age. Everyone seems to *adore* their babies, and
they spoil them and pet them and dress them up beautifully,
but the minute one of the poor little things begins to go to
sleep, they swoop on it and poke it and jog it and throw it in
the air and bandy it about from hand to hand and coo and
chuck and sing, until it is a wonder that any Italian child
survives infancy.

We are both *riddled* with mosquito bites. I've got seven on my face alone, and Pen has had collywobbles today, although she has eaten exactly the same as I have and has stuck more religiously to bottled water. I often lace my Chianti with the Arno (but only in the pensione, where everyone else, French, Italian and English, drink it as a matter of course, and it seems very well filtered).

There are lots of Maltese dogs about, but rather leggy, bad ones.

Monday, 1 September 1947 and Tuesday, 2 September 1947

Both mornings we spent in the Museo di San Marco, which is the monastery in which Fra Angelico lived and worked. The downstairs rooms are full of his paintings and those of his school, and the cells upstairs have each a fresco, some of them by him. The longer you look at the paintings the more heavenly they become. They have a sort of early May morning freshness about them and the people all seem as though, if you watch them a moment more, they will complete the gestures they are making, and you can tell by their faces what they are thinking, particularly in the big deposition from the Cross. We have felt about so many things 'It would have been worth coming to Florence just to see that' – but of the Fra Angelico it is superlatively and utterly true.

We also discovered the peaches during the last two days. For some reason we had only bought figs and grapes before, and the pensione peaches are only middling. But yesterday we bought a couple of the monsters that cover the stalls – each weighing about half a pound, and golden coloured – not believing for a moment that they could be as luscious as they looked – and oh bliss! Oh rapture! Oh poop poop! They are peaches grown in a Fra Angelico Paradise. We ate them in the lovely cloisters, pouring juice in a very vulgar way all over everything.

We had a great bustle this afternoon buying tickets for Siena tomorrow. The bus leaves at six thirty, so we are breakfasting at five thirty, so I'm cutting this short in order to go to bed early.

Oh yes, we went to the cinema last night with our Italian girl. A *very* old, bad, American film, with the people's mouths all talking American, but Italian coming out. We hoped it would be good for our Italian, but really one does have to *have* some Italian before one can improve it. The only words I understood throughout were '*due milioni di dollari*', but the story was easy enough to follow without words.

Wednesday, 3 September 1947

DAMN! It began to rain yesterday evening and it went on and on all night, and at five fifteen this morning, when we were called, a solid tropical wall of water was still descending. We neither of us have macs or umbrellas, and after some debate I decided I couldn't face it – one would have been soaked through and through by the time one reached the bus station, which is about an hour's walk. But the indomitable Pen was not to be deterred, and off she went. Lo and behold, when I woke again at nine – brilliant sparkling sun, which seems as though it's established for the day. I *am* so cross with myself for my sissyness, I bought an umbrella this morning (locking the stable after the horse had gone) and went to the Pitti to see again some special pictures, and this afternoon I am going to sulk up at Fiesole. Signora Rigatti says soothingly, 'It may be raining like anything at Siena' but I don't believe it for moment, how IDIOTIC of me. But coo! It didn't half rain, all the same.

The mistress of the black hen on the roof across from me picks it up and kisses it and coos to it as though it were a puppy, and the hen clucks and croons in return.

I did sulk at Fiesole, and it was so peaceful and lovely in

the Roman ruins, where I stayed all the time, watching the cloud shadows rove over the hills, that I felt quite better afterwards. The tram out broke all records for fullness, even for Italian trams. We stood pressed together, hot body glued to hot body in a squidgy mass, for an interminable thirty minutes, while the poor old tram halted and spluttered up the hill and at every stop people leapt onto the steps and clung to its outside like a swarm of bees. Drama was added to the last five minutes by a large American into whose chest my face was jammed, who announced that he *thought* he might be sick at any moment. We all pleaded with him and threatened and cajoled and implored him to concentrate on the view (which he couldn't possibly see), and luckily all was well.

There was a flock of Swedish students sketching the amphitheatre, who from the distance looked very decorative with their blond heads, but from close up were *so* ugly compared to the Italians. Their legs were either fat or skinny or too short or too long, and their skins were pink and their eyes were piggy. Pen and I have fallen quite in love with the Florentine men. The women are only *fairly* good looking, and some very ugly, but the young men are *so* lovely. It's partly their marvellous colour, but, they are beautifully proportioned too, and the ones that mess about in boats on the

Arno look so very *right* with almost nothing on, compared to skinny, paunchy, hairy naked-looking northerners.

Pen arrived back just as I finished dinner, in very fine form having had a glorious day and picked up a most useful Englishman on the bus, with whom we both went out at once to have drinks. He was such an old bore, really, because he was a photo-fiend, who travels *solely* in order to take photos which he can than show to helpless victims. He was *nice*, and upstanding and presentable (although he was at Keble), but oh those photos. He'd *done* Venice and Florence by that time, but as he printed his pictures himself, he only had the negatives, and there we sat squinting at them against the light for hours and *hours*, exclaiming with such well-simulated rapture that more and *more* came out from his every pocket. We didn't get home till one thirty.

THURSDAY, 4 SEPTEMBER 1947

In the morning we were supposed to be showing Jack Bartley (photo-fiend) the Medici Chapel at San Lorenzo, but of course he went and waited at San Marco instead, so we ended by just looking at it ourselves, and afterwards stumbled, almost by chance, into the Palazzo which has the chapel decorated by Gozzoli with the journey of the three kings. It's small, and each wall is one solid mass of gorgeous, splendiferous colour and detail, and the kings come winding down the hillsides with their retinues, and people hunting in the background – everything so exact and rich and alive, the horses prancing and the hunting cheetahs perched on their cruppers, and the people's faces are portraits of the Medicis, full of life and character. It's luscious.

In the afternoon we took a tram (and a good supply of meringues and sugar cakes) out to Certosa, and went up to the monastery. It was not a very sympathetic monastery – one was shown round by a very firm monk, and only allowed to look at the things he found interesting, and anyway there was nothing much in the way of pictures and the interior architecture was late and disconcertingly like a Regency drawing-room. He was very proud of the refectory tablecloth only being changed once a year – it had been on six months, and I must say it was spotless. We bought tweeny-weeny bottles of liqueur. While we were waiting for the tram home we had orangeades in a very small trattoria, where the locals were so polite that when we finished our drinks and moved to put the glasses on the counter they leapt forward and snatched them from us with a flourish and formal bows,

and we all got tied in knots with our *grazie*s and *prego*s and bows and smiles.

After dinner Jack rang up and there were explanations about the morning and we met for another drink and – believe it or not, *more* photos. Luckily he leaves for Rome at seven a.m. tomorrow. He lives with his mother and sister in South Ken. Gosh! What a frightful week they'll have when he gets home. But I'm sure he's a model son and brother and they'll probably love it and have friends to dinner especially to see his efforts.

Friday, 5 September 1947

I paid my bill this evening so as to know how I stand for last-minute buys and changing lire to francs etc. tomorrow, and find I have ten of my thirty pounds left. That means that including the first three days in the expensive hotel, a fortnight has cost me twenty pounds all in (not counting fare) and of that the pensione has cost just about fifteen shillings a day, including all meals. I've had three baths and three bottles of Chianti (at one shilling each and three shillings each respectively) extra, and they add fifteen per cent for service, and a tax of nearly thirty per cent, for *séjour*, which they all have to pay for each guest. I shall buy something *nice* tomorrow – nylons, or a handbag or something.

We went to Fiesole again this afternoon and saw the monastery there, which is *much* nicer than Certosa, with the cloisters gay with flowers and canaries in aviaries. They are Franciscans. It was a grey day, and looking down on Florence we decided that from above it looks like Letchworth! The view of the other side is much lovelier. Florence definitely *sprawls*, and the cream houses with red roofs might easily be modern blocks of flats. It's only when you are *in* it that it has such glamour and loveliness, and you see the houses in all their delicious irregularity and overhanging eaves and decoratedness and tallness. Of course, we've never seen that view at its best, but only in the afternoon when the sun is in your eyes in that direction, and today there was no sun at all. Afterwards we walked out of Fiesole and climbed a hill among cypresses, trying to find wild anemones (which they are selling in the streets) but failed. There were exquisite little autumn crocuses, though, and the hill was conical so we could see far out all round, and our favourite side, although unadorned by sunshine, was as fascinating as ever with its soft reddish-brown earth and silvery-grey olive orchards, and dark cypresses to keep

it from melting away, and occasional rich green rivulets of acacias.

On reading through this diary I find that I've hardly put in *anything* that we've done. We've really looked at every single church of note in Florence, and climbed the Palazzo Vecchio tower, and spent hours with pictures, and filled our eyes so full of loveliness that they are perfectly dazzled, and all I seem to have written about is pastries. And besides leaving out most of the sight-seeing, which doesn't matter so much, as people's descriptions of beautiful things are always useless, I've left out seeing an Italian (real Italian) film about Venice (v. bad, but rather lush and fun, as Pen and I and Jack each ended up with a different version of the story), and the nice Swedish girls staying here who are very wholesome and remind me of a friend of mine saying on returning from Sweden, 'If the Swedes had ever had anything like Chartres they'd have pulled it down years ago because gargoyles collect dust'. They make me feel very pro-Latin. And I've left out a Maltese who would have ravished Ma who sat up at table with his mistress (a Maltese *dog*) and whose eyebrows were done into neat little plaits tied with blue ribbon. And I've left out Pen's pet carabiniere who told us how to find a Perugino fresco tucked away in a barracks – such a serene and superb

Perugino – and I've left out the *extraordinary* effect of my extremely becoming sun hat on the days I've worn it, which I can only ascribe to the fact that the Florentines think that this lovely weather we have had is *wintry*. A little boy followed me all round a church (when he wasn't sliding down the banister of the pulpit) reaching up and touching the brim behind my back and all the men burst into broad smiles in the street and call after me something of which I can only understand '*Signorina*' and '*cappello*'. As every stall in the straw market is covered with the hats, it couldn't have been because they hadn't seen one before. I really ended up feeling quite shy!

And I really don't feel that I've got in *any* of the general loveliness and charm of everything and everyone. Oh dear!

Saturday, 6 September 1947, Sunday, 7 September 1947 and Monday, 8 September 1947

The last day was the only bad day. I woke with a sore throat which by lunchtime had become a raging feverish cold, and during the morning, I had to lug my suitcase down to the station to register it, only to find that I *couldn't*, as the *dogana* was shut, and wouldn't open again until *after* the train had left next day, and then when I tried to do my last-minute food shopping and delicious buying – lo and behold everything else was shut too, and I gradually discovered that there was a general strike on for the day. The Palazzo Vecchio square and the Uffizi were *packed* with people listening to fiery speeches, but I felt too ill to find out what it was all about. In the after noon I dragged myself out again and did manage to buy a little food, and a reasonably decent jersey from less public-spirited shops, and to get some Swiss and French francs in exchange for my few surplus lire. Then I went to bed.

I was called at six the next morning, and luckily by that time it was clear that it *was* only a cold and not the begin-ning of some frightful disease, so off I plodded to the station, feeling lousy but not desperate, and once there, realised with overwhelming clarity that the sweet dream of getting a *seat* on the train was something to make one *die* laughing. So I stood in the corridor as far as Milan – eight hours. Only actually it wasn't anything like as bad as that sounds. I fought my way through to the part of the corridor belonging to the sleepers, where standing is forbidden, and when driven back by a kind but firm conductor, was able to prove that it was physically impossible for me to go back into my proper sphere, so he allowed me to plant myself just at the very beginning of his territory, where I sat most comfortably on my hatbox, and chatted with a pleasant Swiss girl.

At Milan most of the Italians got out, so I bought a first-class ticket and found an excellent seat in a carriage with a charming Swiss couple and two young Swiss men. We talked French, and I was gratified to find that I could get on admirably. The two young men and I drank a bottle of Chianti, sang and exchanged addresses. They got out halfway through Switzerland, and the remaining three of us spread, and slept comfortably as far as Lausanne, where the Swiss husband got out, leaving his wife and me with a whole side each. (She was going to Paris to see the dress collections.) We were joined later by a rich woman and a bricklayer with a dirty little son, covered with impetigo, who ate all my food and drank all my aqua minerale. I had enough money to eat in the restaurant, and there I picked up an English doctor called Paul Strickland, who arranged to meet me at the Gare de Lyons and see me across Paris. (I *am* really a very talented traveller!) He did that, and we travelled the rest of the way together. I was a bit tired, as the customs and ticket collecting were so arranged as to happen at all the most awkward moments during the night, so that even if one had had a sleeper one wouldn't have had a chance of sleeping much.

We did a clever thing in Paris, and didn't have to change stations – just walked across the platform and there was a train to Calais. There was a lunch car on it too.

The doctor had had a whole month in Italy, and we passed the time in immoderate raptures about it, and its people and everything about it. He'd seen much more of the people than I had, because he talks Italian, and is a great *one* for mixing. We became sadder and sadder, the nearer we got to home. The crossing was rather heaven, all the same. There was a monstrous wind, but for some reason no roll; the boat ploughed along steadily, but every wave that hit it sent a great sheet of sparkling sugar-icing spray over the deck. We stood up in the bow, nearly blown to pieces and ducking under the sort of wall (bulkhead? bulwarks?) every time a wave came, but it was impossible not to get caught out, so that in the end we were soaked. I looked just like Medusa, with stiff writhing snake-locks standing out all round my head, solid with layers of Italian, Swiss and French dirt, overlaid with salt.

We could have got *anything* through the customs. The taxi queue at Victoria was so huge that I rang up for a car, and I reached the flat at about nine o'clock. The journey took three hours less than the journey out. I suppose we made it up at Paris.

So that's the end of that. Oh how I wish it weren't! But still, it's silly to repine, when I've had a holiday which I'll never forget, and which didn't have one unenjoyable minute until the last day (incidentally, the cold is going almost as rapidly as it came, and was already much better by the time I reached Paris), and about which everyone says, 'It must have been marvellous, because you *look* as though you've been enjoying yourself so much.'

I am not brown, nor fatter, and actually today I should think I look rather a wreck, what with the effects of the journey, the cold, and the remaining mosquito bites, but I *feel* quite terrific after it. I really don't think I have ever had such a lovely fortnight in my life.